HUMAN-MADE DISASTERS

PIPELINE ACCIDENTS

BY TRUDY BECKER

WWW.APEXEDITIONS.COM

Apex is distributed by North Star Editions:
sales@northstareditions.com | 888-417-0195

Produced for Apex by Red Line Editorial.

Photographs ©: iStockphoto, cover, 6–7; Shutterstock Images, 1, 4–5, 10–11, 12–13, 14, 15, 16–17, 19, 22–23, 24, 25, 26–27, 29; Amanda Holguin/Carlsbad Current-Argus/AP Images, 8; Brian Kersey/UPI/Alamy, 18; Brett Gundlock/Alamy, 20–21

Library of Congress Control Number: 2023921995

ISBN
978-1-63738-929-4 (hardcover)
978-1-63738-969-0 (paperback)
979-8-89250-064-7 (ebook pdf)
979-8-89250-027-2 (hosted ebook)

Printed in the United States of America
Mankato, MN
082024

NOTE TO PARENTS AND EDUCATORS

Apex books are designed to build literacy skills in striving readers. Exciting, high-interest content attracts and holds readers' attention. The text is carefully leveled to allow students to achieve success quickly. Additional features, such as bolded glossary words for difficult terms, help build comprehension.

TABLE OF CONTENTS

CHAPTER 1

FIERY CAMPSITE

Campers in New Mexico look for a good spot to sleep. They settle under a bridge by the Pecos River. A few hundred yards away, a pipeline lies underground.

Many people camp along the Pecos River every year.

Suddenly, the pipeline bursts open. Natural gas escapes. It catches fire and explodes. Flames fly through the air.

Natural gas catches fire very easily.

FAST FACT

The fire was visible more than 20 miles (32 km) away.

The fire rages for almost an hour. It burns everything it reaches. The explosion also makes a giant **crater**. The land and people are gone.

After pipeline accidents, investigations happen. Groups try to discover the problem with the pipeline. Sometimes, it isn't obvious. Investigations can take years.

The New Mexico explosion happened in August 2000. It killed 12 people.

CHAPTER 2

PIPELINE TROUBLE

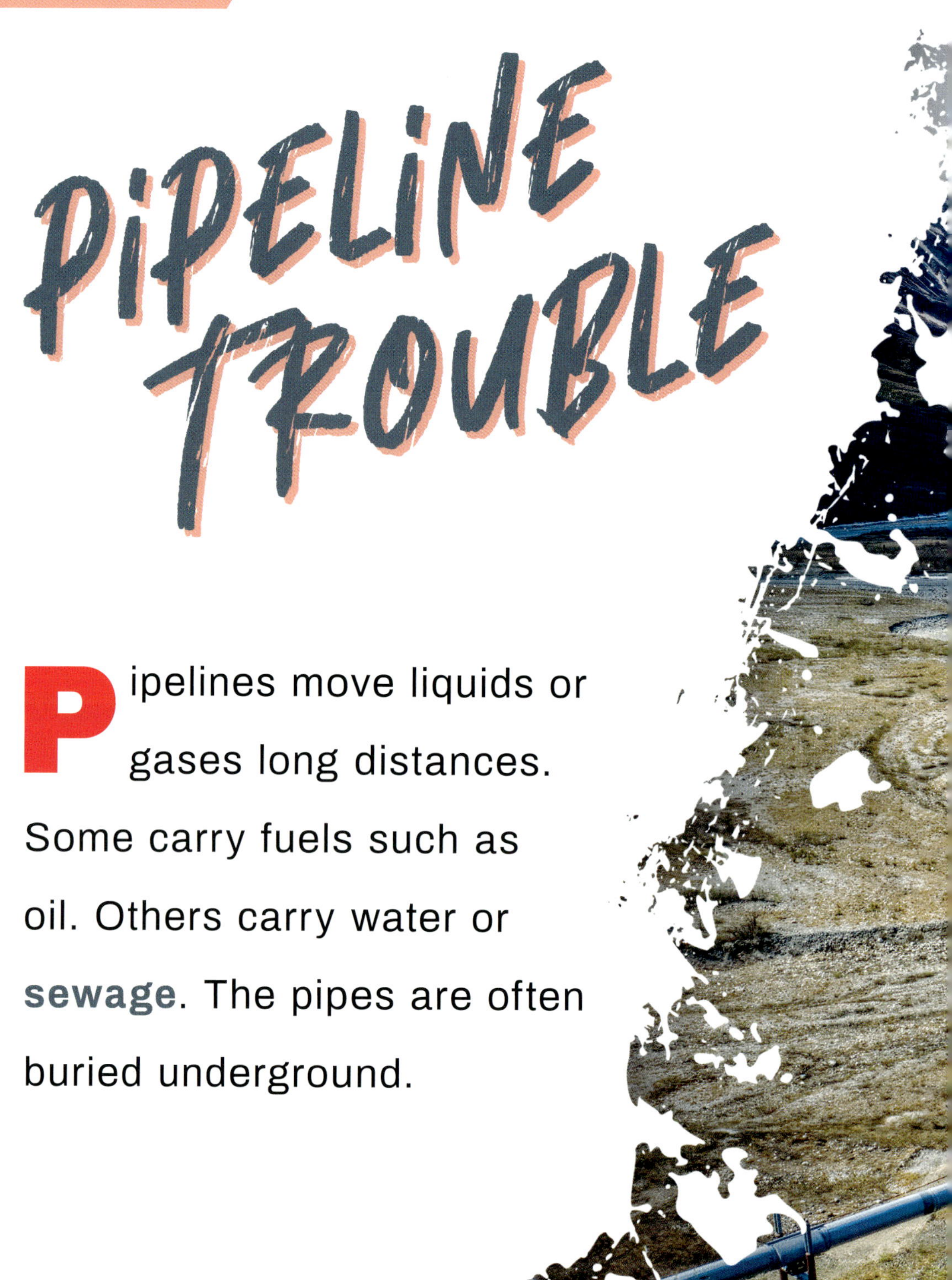

Pipelines move liquids or gases long distances. Some carry fuels such as oil. Others carry water or **sewage**. The pipes are often buried underground.

There are 2.7 million miles (4.3 million km) of pipelines in the United States.

Many pipes are made of metal. If they get wet, they can rust.

Each pipeline has several sections. They are joined together at seams. Sometimes, part of a pipeline breaks. The material inside leaks or bursts out.

CORRODING

Many pipes carry liquid. Wet dirt or rain can also touch pipes. Liquid can make pipes **corrode**. Their sides become thinner and weaker. This makes accidents more likely.

Burning gas and oil spread quickly. Fires can be hard to put out.

Sometimes, the material in pipelines can explode or catch fire. It may also be **hazardous**. As a result, pipeline accidents can hurt many people. They also harm the **environment**.

FAST FACT

Between 2010 and 2018, US pipelines had more than 800 fires.

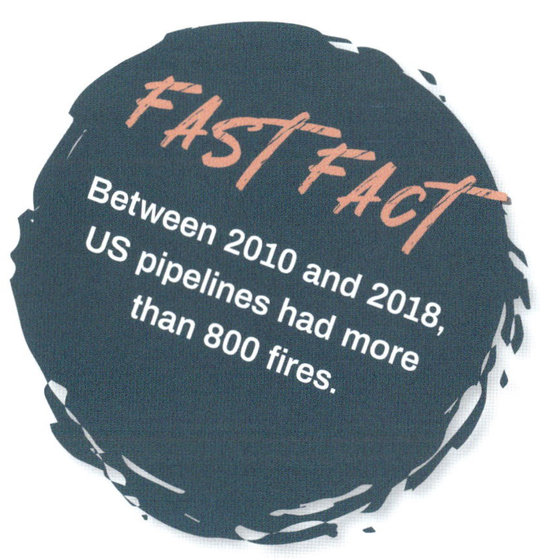

Spilled oil can coat animals' bodies and make them sick.

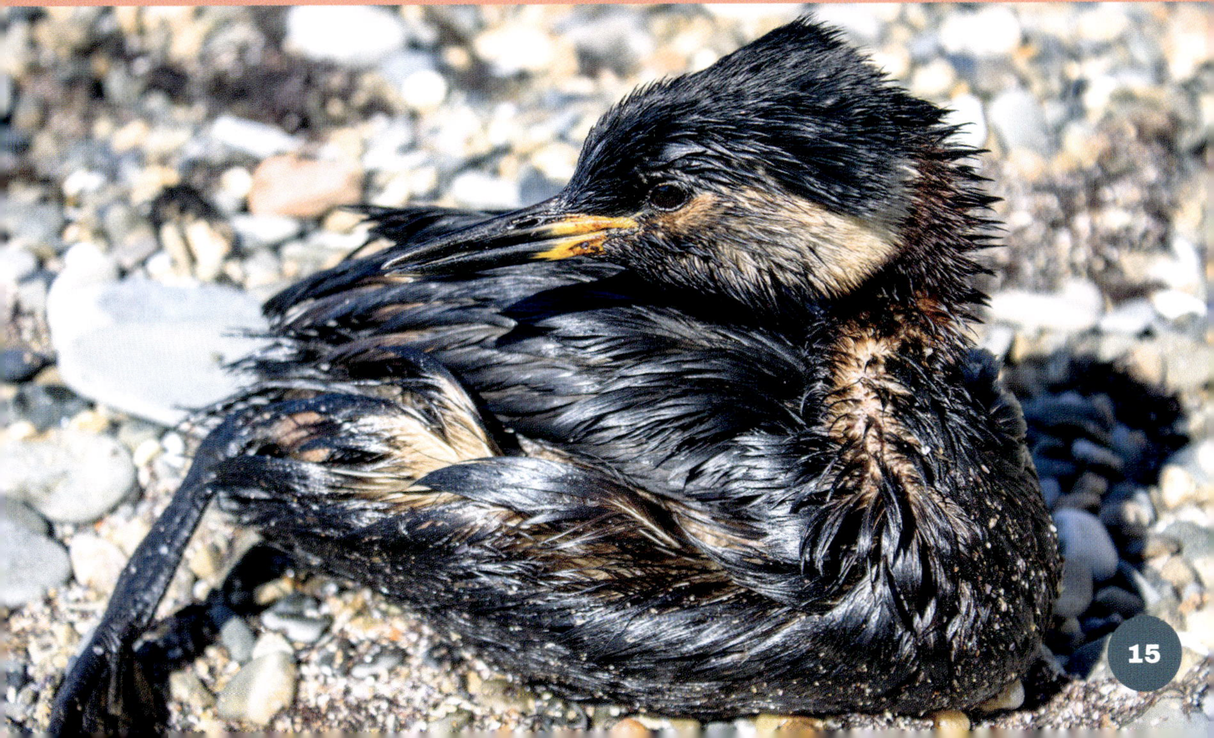

CHAPTER 3

PAST ACCIDENTS

Leaks and spills can be very dangerous. In 1978, gas leaked from a pipe in Mexico. Then it exploded. The blast smashed buildings. It killed 52 people.

Gas leaks often start large fires.

Oil damaged more than 30 miles (48 km) of land along the Kalamazoo River.

In 2010, a pipeline burst in Michigan. Oil poured into the Kalamazoo River. Cleanup took months. It also cost millions of dollars.

PIPELINE PROTESTS

Some people believe pipelines are too risky. The Dakota Access Pipeline is one example. It was planned to go near **Indigenous** lands. People tried to stop it from being built. They held **protests**.

Many people gathered to protest the Dakota Access Pipeline in 2016.

The Keystone pipeline runs through the United States to Canada. It is about 3,000 miles (4,850 km) long.

The Keystone pipeline has carried oil since 2010. It has leaked more than 20 times. One leak took place in December 2022. It let out more than 588,000 gallons (2,226,000 L).

FAST FACT

The 2022 oil spill polluted more than 54 million gallons (204 million L) of water.

CHAPTER 4

After accidents, workers try to put out fires. They also clean up oil or chemicals. But the damage can be very bad. So, preventing accidents is important.

Cleaning up oil spills can take months.

People can repair or replace old pipelines. They can build new, stronger ones. For example, some companies add coatings to pipes and seams. Coated pipes are less likely to break.

Replacing old pipelines can reduce leaks.

LEARNING FROM THE PAST

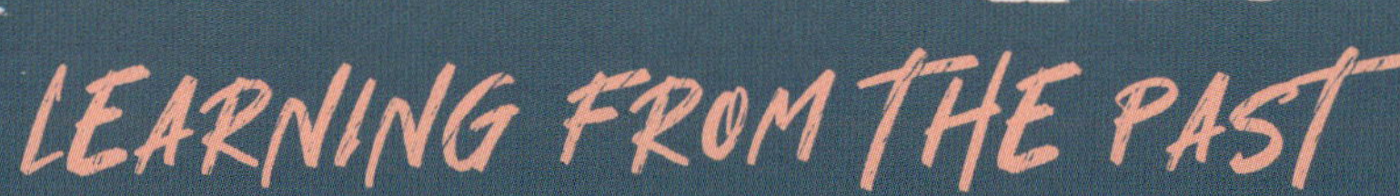

People learn from problems with older pipes. They make new **regulations**. These rules require safer ways of building. That way, accidents are less likely to happen again.

Some regulations say where pipelines can be built. Pipes can't go near important natural areas.

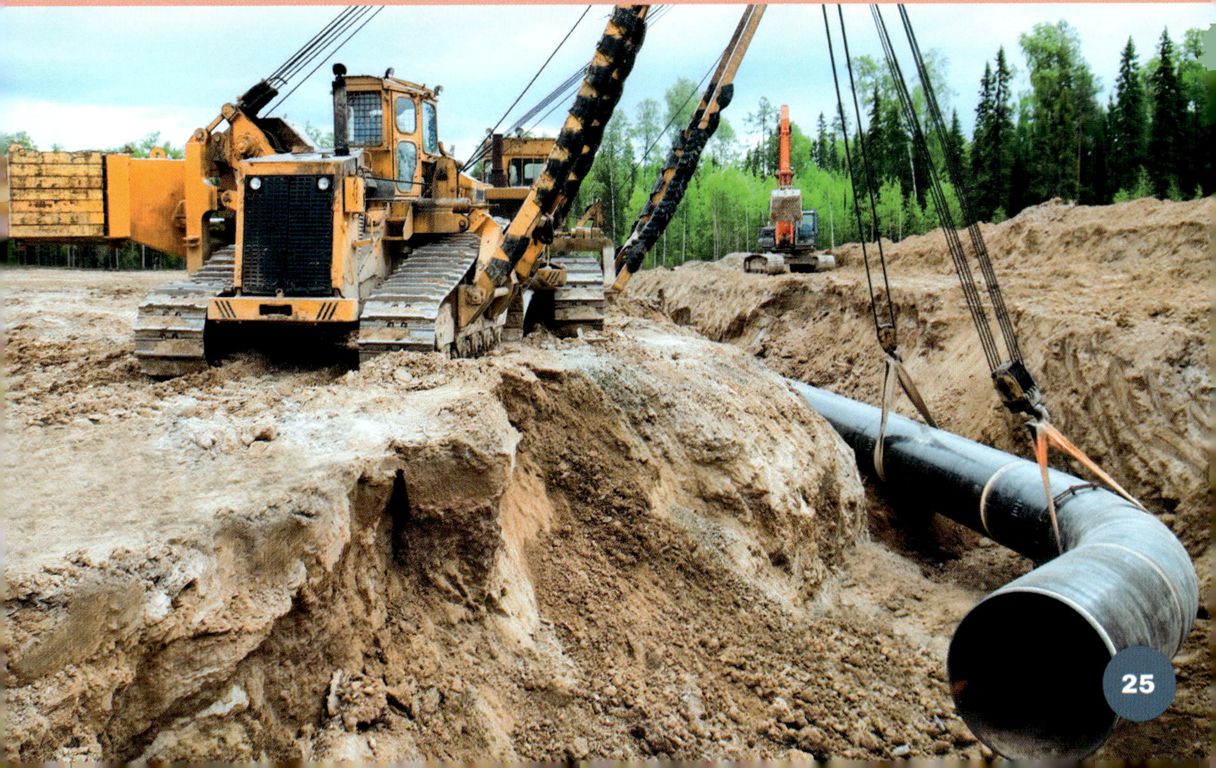

Workers can test joints and seams to make sure they are strong.

Companies test their pipelines, too. That way, they can find and fix problems before accidents happen.

FAST FACT

Workers often test a pipeline's **pressure**. Low pressure can be a sign of leaks or weak spots.

COMPREHENSION QUESTIONS

Write your answers on a separate piece of paper.

1. Write a few sentences explaining the main ideas of Chapter 4.
2. Do you think pipelines are too risky for people to use? Why or why not?
3. When did the Keystone pipeline start carrying oil?
   - **A.** 1978
   - **B.** 2010
   - **C.** 2022
4. Why would corroded pipes make accidents more likely?
   - **A.** Corroded pipes are thicker and stronger.
   - **B.** Corroded pipes are weaker and easier to break.
   - **C.** Corroded pipes make materials move faster.

5. What does **investigations** mean in this book?

After pipeline accidents, ***investigations*** *happen. Groups try to discover the problem with the pipeline.*

A. problems
B. fights
C. studies

6. What does **replace** mean in this book?

People can repair or ***replace*** *old pipelines. They can build new, stronger ones.*

A. put in new versions of
B. break into many pieces
C. keep the same

Answer key on page 32.

GLOSSARY

corrode

To weaken or be worn away.

crater

A bowl-shaped hole made by an explosion.

environment

The natural surroundings of living things.

hazardous

Dangerous.

Indigenous

Related to the original people who lived in an area.

pressure

The amount of force pushing against a pipe from the inside.

protests

Times when people gather to show they disagree with something or call for change.

regulations

Official laws about how something should be done.

sewage

Dirty water that comes from sewers and is full of waste.

BOOKS

Edwards, Sue Bradford. *Investigating Fossil Fuel Pollution*. Mankato, MN: The Child's World, 2022.

Forest, Christopher. *Fossil Fuels.* Minneapolis: Abdo Publishing, 2020.

Simon, Seymour. *Climate Action: What Happened and What We Can Do.* New York: HarperCollins Publishers, 2021.

ONLINE RESOURCES

Visit **www.apexeditions.com** to find links and resources related to this title.

ABOUT THE AUTHOR

Trudy Becker lives in Minneapolis, Minnesota. She likes exploring new places and loves anything involving books.

ANSWER KEY:

1. Answers will vary; 2. Answers will vary; 3. B; 4. B; 5. C; 6. A